Word

Word Play

Language Activities for
Young Children and
Their Parents

Second Edition

Sheila Wolfendale and Trevor Bryans

 David Fulton Publishers   NASEN

David Fulton Publishers Ltd
The Chiswick Centre, 414 Chiswick High Road, London W4 5TF

www.fultonpublishers.co.uk

First published in 1986 by the National Association for Special Educational
Needs (NASEN).
Second edition 1994.
This edition published 2006 in association with NASEN.

10 9 8 7 6 5 4 3 2 1

David Fulton Publishers is a division of Granada Learning Limited

British Library Cataloguing in Publication Data
A catalogue record for this book is available from the British Library.

ISBN: 1 84312 439 4 (EAN: 1 84312 439 9)

Typeset by FiSH Books, Enfield
Printed and bound in Great Britain

Contents

We would like to dedicate this book to the principal author,
Professor Sheila Wolfendale, who sadly passed away in January 2006.

Preface

This book is for practitioners in children's centres, nurseries and infant schools working with children aged 3 to 7 and their parents or carers (hereafter referred to as 'parents'). It provides a framework for a structured programme of language activities and games that can be shared with parents. Alternatively, parents may wish to use the book independently of school, to help their children develop good language skills in readiness for more formal learning at school.

Teachers recognise the importance of a strong working partnership with parents. This book is intended to:

- capitalise on parents' knowledge of their children;
- empower parents to support their children's learning;
- enhance early learning experiences in the home; and
- build foundations for successful learning in school.

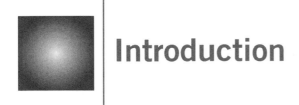

Introduction

Purpose of the book

The purpose of this book is to provide parents and carers with a range of language activities, word games, and story and drama exercises which can be used as the basis of a language programme for young children, with teacher or nursery support. It contains lots of starting points for talking, and for using the time that children and parents spend together creatively. The activities are designed for children aged 3 and 7.

What is a language programme?

In the context of this book the programme can be seen as a series of planned language and learning experiences, tailored to meet the learning needs of an individual child. By prior agreement, the parent undertakes to set aside time for regular sessions with the child at home.

How long should the programme run?

The book gives many examples of language activities. These are not intended to be comprehensive, but rather they can stimulate parent and teacher to develop and expand the ideas. There is enough material in the book for a programme to run for a year. However, parents and staff may wish to plan a programme lasting only a few weeks in the first instance.

What is a session?

Each session should last approximately fifteen minutes and may take place daily or several times a week. There is probably no 'best' time during the day for a session; indeed, some of the sessions will be based around the child's play and other routines which occur naturally during the day. For example, stories often take place just before or at bedtime.

Some of the language activities chosen for the sessions at home may specifically complement experiences the child has had during the day, at nursery, infant school or at a children's centre.

The theory behind the programme

In recent years, teachers, nursery staff and parents have demonstrated that they can work together effectively on behalf of the young children they care for, and they have jointly co-operated on language and early learning programmes. Older children and their parents have also successfully worked on home-based reading programmes under the guidance of teachers. It seems that not only do children make progress in the joint ventures, but also that everyone involved finds them an enjoyable and rewarding experience. (Further details of these ventures can be found in several of the books listed in 'References and suggested further reading' at the end of the book.)

Research has specifically indicated that parent–child dialogue is a particularly powerful way of developing the child's intellect. Indeed, there is plenty of evidence to suggest that only with considerable language input and support from their parents are children likely to achieve their full intellectual potential.

Major reports into children's development and education have suggested that planned intervention in the children's language by teachers and parents should be a priority. We now know, too, that early language stimulation is a powerful precursor to learning to read.

In recognition of these principles and research findings, the government has encouraged the introduction of 'family literacy' initiatives. These involve children, parents and other family members in developing an appreciation and enjoyment of spoken and written language, encouraging conversation and fostering early reading skills (see opposite). Many schools have family literacy schemes as part of their implementation of the National Literacy Strategy and this book will support their work.

What teachers and parents can offer each other

Teachers are trained to match their knowledge of child development with their knowledge of educational principles and the curriculum in order to plan and provide educational experiences for children. They have the advantage of an

Literacy all around us

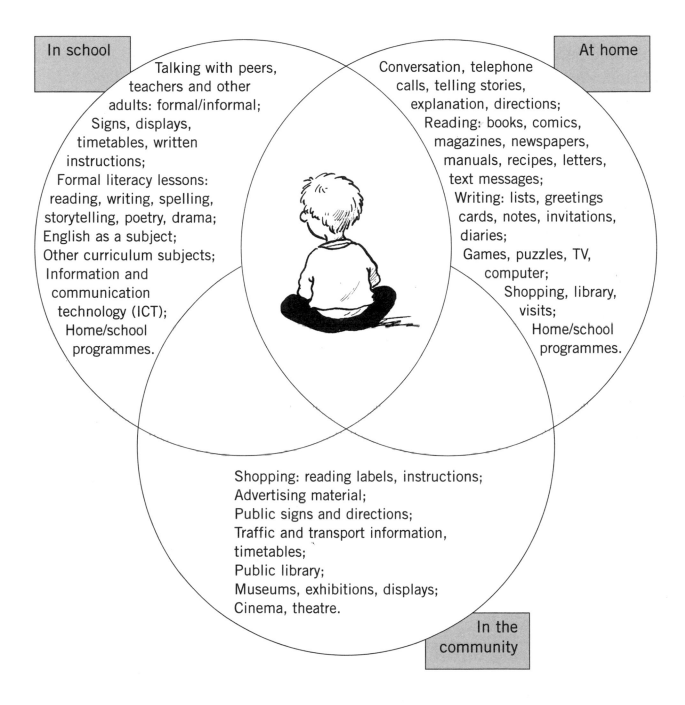

In school

Talking with peers, teachers and other adults: formal/informal;
Signs, displays, timetables, written instructions;
Formal literacy lessons: reading, writing, spelling, storytelling, poetry, drama;
English as a subject;
Other curriculum subjects;
Information and communication technology (ICT);
Home/school programmes.

At home

Conversation, telephone calls, telling stories, explanation, directions;
Reading: books, comics, magazines, newspapers, manuals, recipes, letters, text messages;
Writing: lists, greetings cards, notes, invitations, diaries;
Games, puzzles, TV, computer;
Shopping, library, visits;
Home/school programmes.

In the community

Shopping: reading labels, instructions;
Advertising material;
Public signs and directions;
Traffic and transport information, timetables;
Public library;
Museums, exhibitions, displays;
Cinema, theatre.

© Sheila Wolfendale and Trevor Bryans (2006) *Word Play: Language Activities for Young Children and Their Parents*. David Fulton Publishers

accumulating store of professional wisdom as the backcloth to their daily practice. Parents contribute their life experience as well as knowledge of their own child's development and individual characteristics. They also have the advantage of intimate daily contact with their child. Parents offer emotional support and protection to their children as well as providing a safe environment in which development can take place. This support enables young children to explore the world. They are seen by their children to be influential and knowledgeable when making decisions. So the experience and skills that each adult brings to a joint enterprise complement the child's learning.

Reason for selecting the language activities

Researchers have investigated the verbal exchanges between parents and young children occurring naturally in the home. Some of this parent–child discourse is particularly intensive and intellectually stimulating for the child because parent and child are simultaneously focused on the same task. It is for this level of the parent–child discourse that the language activities in the book have been selected. The conversation activities mirror many of the child's experiences in the school or nursery setting.

The activities have been arranged into nine chapters which together reflect a range of functions in language and communication. Inevitably, many of the activities overlap because, as yet, there is no established order of teaching or acquiring language competence. It is for this reason that we have, intentionally, not laid out a rigid format or sequence to be followed; rather we have attempted to provide material from which programmes for individual children could be drawn by the adults concerned. There is ample scope for flexibility by including timely or current experiences in the child's life.

Stages in carrying out a language programme

In the publications already referred to and listed at the end of this book, we can find overwhelming evidence to support the view that intervention is more effective if it is jointly planned at the outset and reviewed frequently by parent and teacher thereafter. Below is one possible way of proceeding through the various stages of setting up and carrying out a language programme.

Stage 1: Preparation

The decision to introduce a language programme may come about as part of a parental involvement programme that already exists in the nursery, children's centre or school. So members of staff and parents may already be sharing information about children and may agree that a particular child or small group of children would benefit. Of course, more than one member of staff can be involved. Some settings have a staff member with responsibility for home liaison, and this person can lead the language programme project.

The first meeting between parent(s) and staff will be to discuss the overall purpose of the language programme and then to agree to carry out the following steps within a timescale:

(a) Parent and teacher arrange to meet again to share their knowledge of the child's language and interests in terms of the following guidelines:

> What does the child like doing best at home/nursery?
>
> Who does the child talk to most at home/nursery?
>
> Does the child enjoy listening to stories and talking about them?
>
> Does the child enjoy reciting nursery rhymes and songs?
>
> Does the child take picture and storybooks out from the nursery/local library?

Encourage the parent to provide detail where possible, rather than reply with one-word answers. It is suggested that a written record be kept of the discussion, for example using a form such as the one shown overleaf. Use the discussion and the written record to detail those activities in this book which will form the basis of the language programme.

(b) Agree immediate priority activities to begin with and a provisional, longer-term set of activities.

(c) Decide tentatively how long the programme ought to last.

(d) Agree how often to meet to review or modify the programme.

(e) Agree on ways of collecting and compiling other materials (pictures, objects, stories, rhymes, paper or other aids) for the sessions.

Stage 2: Carrying out the programme

Once the programme has begun, the parent agrees to keep a written record, using a format such as the one shown on pages 7 and 8. This will be the main means of communication between teacher and parent and can be a valuable tool if completed appropriately.

5

Introductory meeting between parent and teacher

Parent's name: Teacher's name:

Child's name: Child's DoB:

Date of meeting:

What does the child like doing best at home/nursery?

Who does the child talk to most at home/nursery?

Does he/she enjoy:

Listening to stories

talking about stories/TV programmes/events of the day

joining in with nursery rhymes and songs

looking at picture books

talking about picture books

Record Card

Child's name: ....

Name of nursery/school: ....

Week no: .... Week ending: ....

Day	Book section	Activity	Parent's comments

Teacher's comments:

Record Card

Child's name: Ben Robinson

Name of nursery/school: High Cross Nursery

Week no: 1   Week ending: 10th October

Day	Book section	Activity	Parent's comments
Mon	1	Looking in mirror	We stood at the mirror in the bedroom and compared our hair and eyes and how tall. Ben liked this – he copied most of what I said.
Tues			Ben was keen to get in front of the mirror again. He pointed to his eyes and said 'Blue eyes'. We played for 10 minutes and I asked him to show me arm, leg, hand, foot, knee. I had to show him 'knee' but he knew the rest.
Thurs		Abby was here to play so we all played 'simon says'	Both kids loved this game– I put on some music. Ben copied Abby at first but by the end he could do all the actions – Wave your arms, stamp your feet, shake your hands, bend your legs.

Teacher's comments:

Ben was very unsure about the names of different parts of the body and so this is good progress. He is sometimes very shy in nursery and doesn't like to join in group games like this, so getting him to do it at home is very good social training.

Try to get Ben to do the calling out for 'simon says' next week. When you think he is ready, add new words one at a time – ankle, elbow, neck etc.

Well done both of you! ☺

The comments section is particularly important as the parent can provide information about:

- how easy or difficult the child found the activity;
- if the activity had to be repeated;
- how the child responded, i.e. whether he/she was settled or restless, interested or indifferent;
- the parent's own response to the session;
- issues to do with the level of difficulty of the activities;
- family factors that affect the running of the programme.

Some parents are not confident about this type of record keeping, so showing them an example can be useful. If it proves to be a burden to the parent suggest that they simply record the activity and use a smiley/sad face in the comments column.

It is suggested that the parent returns the completed record card at the end of each week and the teacher adds weekly summary comments covering:

- his/her overall response to information provided by the parent;
- his/her comments on how the child has been at school/nursery during the week, what activities he/she has engaged in, enjoyed, and so on.

Stage 3: Measuring progress

There are two main ways of evaluating a programme to establish if it is working. These are to consider:

- Is the child making progress in language competence?
- Are the parent(s) and staff satisfied with the progress made and the ways in which it is organised and running?

Assessment of a programme ranges from subjective qualitative judgement (e.g. 'John seems much happier and is talking more with both staff and other children') to much tighter, precise measures of the child's achievement of specific language behaviour. There are advantages and disadvantages with all forms of evaluation. Some methods are listed below.

Behavioural approaches

The most stringent form of evaluation, which we recommend be carried out with advice and help from support personnel such as advisory teachers or educational psychologists, is that which forms part of a behaviourally oriented language programme. For some children, staff and parents may feel that it is important to have more clearly defined teaching goals in the form of target objectives in particular areas of language performance and that there should be an agreed period of time over which progress towards these goals should be made.

In the context of this book, the target objective is a statement about a child's observable language behaviour, stating the conditions under which this behaviour occurs and the standard which a child has to achieve. For example, if the teacher and parent record on a language observation form that a child is restless and fidgety during story-time and is not listening to the story, then an appropriate target objective might be:

> 'By the end of the autumn term, John will be able to answer three questions about a story he has chosen for his mother to read to him at home.'

In this case the measurement of progress is in terms of whether or not the objective has been achieved.

Test and checklist

If the programme is run for a period of six months or more, it is possible to use a test at the outset (pre-test) and again at the end (post-test) to assess progress. For these purposes a variety of language tests is available which can be carried out by advisory teachers, educational psychologists and speech therapists in co-operation with the teacher or nursery nurse. A developmental language checklist, compiled on the basis of continuous observation in the nursery setting, could be used to measure the child's developing language competence.

Record keeping

The record card described above in Stage 2 can be used to keep cumulative records. The teacher or nursery nurse may wish to transfer details of activities carried out from the weekly record card completed by the parent on to a monthly summary chart as a longer-term means of checking on the balance of the activities in relation to the child's language needs and to assist in forward planning. The parent should be given a copy. Opposite is an example of a partially compiled monthly summary chart. This format can be varied or broken down still further.

Monthly Summary Chart

Child's name: ....

Name of nursery/school: ....

Month ending: ....

Activities	Week 1	Week 2	Week 3	Week 4
Puppets	●●		●	
Storytelling	●	●●		●
Conversation time				
Five senses			●●	
Awareness of time	●	●		

Comments:

Progress review meetings

It is suggested that short, regular review meetings be held every two or three weeks. At these, teacher/staff and parent(s) can discuss:

● progress to date;

● any difficulties in organisation;

● any necessary modification to programme content or presentation.

Talking with children

There is a lot that adults can do to help children develop language skills. A number of 'common sense' strategies are set out as 'Key points' below (1–4) and in Chapter 2 (5–6).

Key points 1

Planning sessions

● Find somewhere comfortable where you can both be close and where you will not be interrupted.

● If possible, agree with the child in advance the best time for a session and protect the time chosen; but be flexible – catch your child at a receptive moment.

● Don't make the session too long, and be prepared to stop if the child is bored or distressed.

● Check that you have any materials needed before you start.

● Explain the purpose of the session to other family members.

● Check that you have the materials needed.

● Explain the purpose of the session to other family members.

Key points 2

Talking with your child

- Don't set out to teach – the aim is not to prove that you know more than the child.

- Establish the habit of looking directly at the child when talking; eye contact promotes good communication.

- Ensure that the child does most of the talking.

- Take turns as much as possible.

- Ask questions which 'open' a discussion, not 'close' it.

Example of an 'open' question: 'What's the postman doing in the picture?' Give the child a chance to offer comment, explanation and description.

Example of a 'closed' question: 'Is the boy swimming?' These questions usually invite 'yes/no' answers.

Questions should enable the child to respond in different ways, not just to give 'right' answers.

Key points 3

Praising and correcting

- Repeat back to your child a slow and clear version of any indistinct speech he/she utters.

- Repeat back a corrected version of any grammatical errors, for example:

  Child: He runned fast.

  Adult: Yes, he ran very fast, didn't he?

- Get into the habit of responding to an incorrect statement from your child by giving the correct word, for example: 'Mmmm . . . is it a cow, or is it a horse do you think?'

Key points 4

The most important requisites of all are:

- Be relaxed.

- Enjoy the sessions: talking and learning can and should be fun for you and your child.

1 | Conversation time

This chapter provides lists of conversation topics on everyday events and matters in the life of a young child. A few minutes conversation on any chosen topic allows the parent and child to explore ideas and facts, make associations, comparisons and acquire information. This shared time confirms to the child that adults are a valuable source of information about the world. For the parent the dialogue can be equally rewarding as an opportunity to find out more about the child's thinking. All the activities are intended to give the child a greater sense of self.

Myself and my family

Physical appearance

Talk about each other's appearance – look in a mirror.

'My hair is short. Your hair is curly.'

Parts of the body

- Examine and talk about different parts of the body, size and shape of hands, how joints bend, what body parts are for. Ask the child to name a part of the body.

    'Let's start with our heads and go downwards to our toes, naming as many parts of our bodies as we can.'

- Give the child some clues to different parts of the body and tell the child that you want them to try to guess what they are. For example:

    'These help you to see.'
    'These help you to hear.'
    'You have five of these on each hand.'

'These grow on the ends of your fingers.'
'You have five of these on each foot.'
'These grow on the ends of your toes.'
'This helps you to smell.'
'This helps you to talk.'
'This helps you to breathe.'
'This helps you to throw a ball.'
'This helps you to kick a ball.'
'These cover your eyes when you sleep.'
'These help you to bite your food.'
'These help you to hold a pencil.'
'This bends when you touch your head.'
'This bends when you walk upstairs.'

● Take turns in giving instructions (this can be played as a 'Simon says' game). For example:

'Close your eyes; open your eyes; stand up; sit down; stand on one foot; hold up your hand; hold up two hands; put your hands down; hold your nose; touch your head; now hold your nose and rub your tummy; put one hand on your head and the other on your tummy; now turn round very slowly; with one hand touch your nose, mouth, chin, knee; clap your hands once; now twice; now three times.'

● Say 'I am becoming very, very small.' Demonstrate this and ask the child to bend as low as possible, or to curl up on the floor. Then take it in turns to:

'Touch your nose with one hand; touch your mouth with your elbow (Try!); touch your feet with both hands; touch your hair with one thumb; take one step forward; now take two steps back; now stand very tall again; now shrink and become very small.'

● Then say:

'I am going to say a part of your body, and as I say it, I want you to touch it – I shall say the word quite fast, so listen very carefully: head, tummy, elbow, feet, ankle, eyes, ears, neck, back, hair, shoulders, cheek.'

This can be repeated varying the order of the words, and/or the speed, to suit the child.

- Play 'O'Grady says'. For example:

  O'Grady says:

  'Hold your hand behind your back.'
  'Put your feet together.'
  'Clap your hands three times.'
  'Stand with your feet apart.'
  'Sit on the floor.'
  'Hands on head.'
  'Touch your toes.'
  'Fold your arms.'
  'Stand on tiptoe.'
  'Stand on one leg.'
  'Clap you hands four times.'
  'Crawl on all fours/hands and knees.'
  'Clench your fists tightly.'
  'Sit on the floor.'
  'Stretch your arms as high as you can.'
  'Clap your hands twice.'

- Use two parts of the body at the same time and describe the activity, for example, rub wrist on leg, scratch back with fingers, put lips on hand.

Basic details of self

Parent and child, together, list basic information, such as:

- child's name, address, age, date of birth/birthday, school
- details of other family members, brothers, sisters, other close relations such as uncles, aunts, grandparents, close friend.

Family details

- The parent shares information and stories about family members with the child.
- A longer-term project would be to compile family histories by collecting photographs, asking family members to discuss events in their lives with the child, and weaving stories around a family object or household items.

Making maps

● Parent and child draw simple maps/plans of:

a room in the home, showing furniture, door, window (for example see Figure 1.1);

their home, showing different rooms; upstairs and downstairs;

their garden;

their street, where their home is, and showing where friends and neighbours live;

the neighbourhood, showing the child's school, library, shops and park.

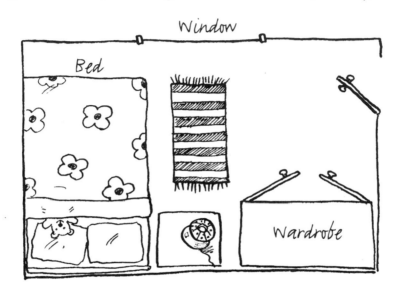

FIGURE 1.1 A plan of Kelly's bedroom

- Ask the child to give you (or Teddy, or an imaginary visitor) directions to a friend's home, shops, school, park. What is the best way to get there? On foot, by bus, by train, by boat?

All about me

What I can do

Parent and child talk about each skill (see overleaf). Tick off what has been learned and discuss what needs to be practised next.

Likes/dislikes

Talk about the child's likes and dislikes in different aspects of their life, for example:

- play/games: 'What do you like to play with? What are your favourite toys/games?';
- favourite activities (outings, visits, treats, meeting people);
- moods (what makes him/her happy, sad, cry, cross, worried, cheerful);
- school and friends.

Encourage the child to explain and tell you more:

'Who is your friend?'

'Who do you like to play with in the playground?'

'Who do you like to sit with when you do your work/read your books/ do your sums/play in the Home Corner?'

'Who do you like to have your lunch/dinner with?'

'Which friend is kind to you?'

'Which friend makes you laugh?'

'Which friend makes you cross, or angry?'

'Which friend gets you into trouble?'

'Which friend helps you with your work?'

'Which friend talks to you most?'

'Who pushes you or fights with you?'

'Who likes you best?'

What I can do

- fasten and unfasten buttons

- do up my zip

- wipe and blow my nose.

- use a knife to cut and spread

- get dressed and undressed

- brush my teeth

- brush and comb my hair

- wash my face

- take a bath

- tie my shoelaces

- put away my toys and clothes

- go to the toilet and wash my hands

Any one of these questions could be followed up with a 'Why' question, for example: 'Why do you like to play with...?'

Other topics for conversation time

Television programmes

Discuss each other's favourite TV programme. Watch a programme together and talk about what happens. Ask questions like:

'How do you think he feels now?'

'Why do you think he was sad at the end?'

Food

Ask the child:

'Let's think of food we eat for breakfast/lunch/dinner/tea.'
'What sort of fruit do you like? Let's think of as many fruits as we can.'
'Where can we buy fruit?' 'Where does it grow?' 'When do we eat it?'
'Where do we buy groceries?'
'Let's think of as many sweet things to eat as we can.'
'Let's think of as many savoury things to eat as we can.'

Ask children to describe their favourite foods (the name, type, colour, texture, taste).

Clothing

Ask the child:

> 'What clothes do you wear to go to bed/swimming/out to play/to school?'

> 'What are these clothes called?' Hold up various garments or point to them on the washing-line

> 'What clothes would you wear to go out in the snow/rain?' 'Why?'

> 'What kind of materials are summer/winter clothes made of?'

> 'What clothes would you wear at the beach on a sunny day?'

Housework

Say to the child:

> 'Let's think of as many types of housework as we can.' (dusting, sweeping, polishing, wiping, mopping, vacuuming, brushing, cleaning)

Ask the child to explain what these activities are and their purpose. Can the child mime the actions to illustrate their verbal explanations? Parents and child take turns to mime a cleaning action, to be guessed by the other. Other questions on this topic include:

> 'What would happen if we didn't do . . . ?' (for example, the dusting)

> 'Who does the housework?' (Use this opportunity to talk about different roles in the family.)

Carrying out other tasks around the house

The parent asks: 'What do we need to:

> make a bed?
> bake a cake?
> clean shoes?
> wash clothes?
> write a story?'

Parent and child discuss the materials needed as well as the order of carrying out these tasks.

Means of travel

The parent asks the child:

'We travel to school. We travel to work. Where else do we travel?'

'What do we use to travel?'

'Can you finish these sentences?

We walk to school on our...

Something we travel in that has four wheels and an engine, is called a...

Something we can travel in on rails is called a... It has lots of...

Something we can travel on that has two large wheels, handle-bars, no engine, is called a...

People who are very ill, or injured, travel to hospital by...

Something we travel in on the water can be a...

Something that travels under the sea can be a...

Something which travels on the roads that can carry many passengers is called a...

Something that travels in the air that carries passengers to other countries is called a...'

Places to live

Ask the child:

'Let's think of some kinds of homes people live in.' (house, flat/apartment, bungalow, cottage, mansion, terraced house, villa, maisonette, castle, palace...)

'What is a house?' Encourage extended answers.

'Why do we need to live in houses?' (Talk about protection from the cold, rain and excessive heat.)

'Let's think of some places where animals live, and have their homes.' (beehive, rabbit warren, dog kennel)

Events of the day

Parent and child discuss events of the day, perhaps using a simple diary. This will include getting up, going to school, coming home, having tea, going to bed.

Weather and seasons

Parent and child discuss daily weather, for example: a windy day, frost on a roof, warm evenings, dew on the grass, rain or snow.

Events of the day

2 | Storytelling

Parents have been telling stories to their children from time immemorial. There are many benefits to be gained from this activity:

- helping a child to unwind and relax, particularly at the end of the day;
- fostering closeness between parent and child;
- providing the child with a secure base from which to learn about and absorb new experiences;
- encouraging children to listen to words and their meanings;
- developing and expanding vocabulary and language skills;
- stimulating curiosity.

Sources for stories

Stories can be about anything and everything. They can be drawn from the child's and family's daily experience. They can be folk and fairytales, myth, legend, fantasy, history, adventure, tales from other lands, tales of animals or pets, as well as humorous or nonsense stories.

Format for stories

Stories can be:

- invented by parent or child, or by both together taking it in turns;
- made up about a picture, object, animal or person;
- read by the parent to the child;
- retold time and again.

Stories and accompanying activities

If stories are part of a teacher–parent planned project, there are a number of activities which can support and enhance the storytelling. Here are some suggestions:

- Tape or write the story.
- Parent and child try to anticipate what will happen next in the story.
- Repeat parts of a story, for effect; use different voices and sound effects.
- Ask the child to retell the story.
- Help the child's understanding by discussing the story. Ask questions about the characters: 'How do you think Sam felt when he fell into the pond?'
- Take it in turns to ask questions about the story.
- Re-enact the story – puppets could be used.
- Draw or paint the events and characters.
- If the story is based on the child's own experience, discuss details and ask 'What if…?' questions.
- Invent a sequel to the story.

Key points 5

Storytelling

- If follow-up work is to be included in the session, keep the story short.

- Ensure that the child is relaxed, comfortable and can see and handle materials (books, pictures) easily.

- It helps children to realise that writing and print goes from left to right across the page and that written words have meaning. So from time to time it is good idea to follow words in the story by pointing at them.

- Develop skills of reading stories and storytelling such as:

    (a) reading aloud with expression and intonation

    (b) varying expression (facial and vocal), especially for different characters in a story

    (c) using accompanying gestures where appropriate.

Action rhymes

Clap your hands, clap your hands
One, two, three
Pat your hands, pat your hands
On your knees
Now stretch your arms high
Reach for the sky
Clap, clap, clap
Away they fly . . .
(Follow the actions as described)

The elephant walks like this and that
(Slow lumbering walk, rocking from side to side)
He's terribly tall
(Stretch arm up high)
And terribly fat
(Hold hands out wide)
He's got no fingers
(Wiggle fingers)
He's got no toes
(Touch toes)
But goodness gracious, what a nose!
(Wave arm in front of face like a trunk)

Eight little fingers standing up tall,
Two big ears to hear the birds call,
One runny nose to blow and blow,
Ten little toes in a wriggly row,
Two fat thumbs that wiggle up and down,
Two little feet to stamp on the ground,
Hands to clap and eyes to see,
This is you and this is me.
(Follow the actions as described)

I'm a little teapot, short and stout.
(Bend knees and put arms out)
This is my handle and here is my spout.
(Put one hand on hip for handle, the other curled out for the spout)
When you want a cup of tea, hear me shout . . .
'Tip me up and pour me out'.
(Rock sideways).

Rhymes and songs

Teachers and parents may agree to include nursery rhymes and action songs in some of the sessions (see p. 27 for a few examples). These are a source of immense fun for the children and parents alike and are also a sound basis for learning, since they involve listening, repetition, anticipation, word play, humour and imagination. (You can find a good selection of nursery rhyme books and tapes in your local library.)

Key points 6

Rhymes and songs

- This is a joint activity, rather than an opportunity for 'teaching'; the aim is to share the experience of language.

- Take turns in reciting or singing.

- Provide a wide choice of rhymes and songs, including home-made ones.

- There is no need to correct substitutions or omissions in the child's version of a rhyme.

- If the child hesitates or cannot anticipate the next word, gently prompt with the initial sound or say the word.

Puppets

Puppets are traditionally part of childhood and are an essential part of play. They can be used as the medium for interpreting and anticipating real-life situations, and thus help children to prepare for new experiences and for problem-solving. Puppets can act as models of behaviour which a child can reject, imitate or identify with.

The use of puppets helps with the development of:

- comprehension and expression of language;
- competence in communicating and conveying emotion and feeling;

- visual and auditory attention;
- listening;
- social skills, social comprehension and empathy;
- positive self-concept.

Suitable puppets include finger, glove, home-made rod puppets and marionettes. (Simple puppets can be very effective, for example a face on a paper bag or a face painted on a hand using the thumb and first finger as a mouth.) With very little practice, it is possible to carry out the following (these are only examples):

- **physical actions**: standing, sitting, swimming, driving, cycling, somersaulting, waving, conducting, beckoning, arms folded, saluting, holding objects, falling, drinking, hitting, throwing, stroking, kissing, nodding/shaking head, shaking with laughter;
- **expressions of feeling**: sad, crying, happy, proud, cross, upset, curious, shy, frightened, stubborn, thinking or doubting (by stroking chin).

Puppets can be used to encourage a child's development in the following areas.

Anticipating new experiences

Pretend that the puppet is: going to the doctor, dentist, into hospital; worrying about the birth of a baby in the family; moving house; going to a new school; visiting and making friends.

Problem-solving

Use the puppet to show how to tackle some problem-solving activities, for example: hiding and finding; 'I spy'; thinking; counting and sorting; sorting by shape, colour, size.

Comprehension and vocabulary building

To encourage development of comprehension and to build vocabulary use the puppet for the following activities:

puppet mimes an action and the child has to guess what the puppet is doing; naming of objects and body parts;

miming short story sequences (puppet as child's companion);

puppet and child looking at books and pictures;

puppet re-enacts features of the day.

Expression of emotions

As well as using the puppet to portray emotions, this is an opportunity for a child to express his/her own feelings via the medium of a puppet. Initially, this may need encouragement, example and practice.

Emotions (such as those listed above under 'Expressions of feeling') can be used as an accompaniment to stories or recounted experiences.

Social skills and sensitivity

Use the puppet to express different feelings (using gestures as listed above) and ask the child to guess the puppet's mood. Follow this with guided questioning by the adult about cause and effect and consequences. In this way social rules can be demonstrated via puppet play.

3 | Expression of feelings and social awareness

Activities in this section aim to:

- encourage the child to express feelings and thoughts;
- heighten social awareness;
- increase social communication and social sensitivity skills; and
- develop empathy.

Play and drama

In play, children spontaneously create their own dramatic situations and reconstructions of reality. Play can also help the child to work through and express emotional conflicts. This can be achieved in a variety of ways, all of which will involve matching the child's areas of difficulty with a suitable activity.

Expression of emotion

- Ask the child to show different kinds of emotion: happiness, sadness, surprise, anger, pain, love, disappointment. Parent and child take turns and each has to identify the emotion portrayed.
- Set up a role-play sequence where one person gives a present to another; the one receiving the present shows surprise, pleasure, excitement, puzzlement (what is it?) or disappointment. Talk about not always showing our true feelings – for example, when Grandma gives you a DVD that you've already got.

Spontaneous storytelling

The parent begins a story and the child puts his/her own ideas into it.

Adult: Jake was going to nursery school one morning feeling very sad, because ...

Child: I know – because his mummy is in hospital.

Adult: OK...Jake was going to nursery school one morning feeling very sad, because his mummy is in hospital. But when he gets to nursery, he cheers up because...

The adult may need to help out with suggestions until the child gets the hang of things.

Responding to music

- The parent can ask the child to listen to short pieces of music and to say whether the music sounds sad, happy.
- Parent and child listen to different short pieces of music and move around the room according to the mood of the music – expressing themselves in whatever way they want.

Social sensitivity training

The following activities can be used to develop social sensitivity skills.

The meaning of gestures

Discuss and illustrate with the child the meaning of various gestures, such as waving goodbye, shaking a fist, wagging a finger, turning away, outstretched arms in gestures of welcome.

Tones of voice

Parent and child listen to different voices demonstrating different emotions, and identify these (in the course of watching a TV programme, or the adult using different tones of voice for the characters in a story).

Facial expressions

Collect pictures of faces. Parent and child identify the expressions or emotions depicted.

Making social judgements

Tell or read to the child an incomplete story which involves social judgement of an outcome. The child anticipates or supplies the story's ending, such as: being late for a party, being rude to a teacher, hitting a small boy or girl, finding something a friend has lost.

Discussions involving cause and effect

The parent asks the child to tell them what they think in the following situations:

- Why?: 'Can you tell me why:

    Daddy gets upset when his car doesn't start in the morning?

    Mummy gets cross when the cat brings in a dead bird?

    Teacher sometimes shouts at the class?

    Dad is happy on Sundays?'

- If: 'What would you do if:

    you lost 50p on the way home from the shops?

    a boy smaller/bigger than you hit your little brother?

    your friends wouldn't play with you?

    you had a bag of sweets and you saw your friend?'

- Because:

    'The teacher was cross with Jimmy because . . .'

    'When Jenny got home from school her mum was laughing because . . .'

    'Peter's little sister hit him because . . .'

    'Parminder felt happy because . . .'

- What happend then:

    'Colin broke the window with a stone. What happened then?'

    'Kuli took some money from Jamie's pocket. What happened when she found out?'

The parent should encourage elaboration on each theme.

Use stories and fables

To promote understanding of co-operation, social fairness and the development of initiative, use stories and fables.

Co-operative games

Co-operative games have enormous value for children as they can teach patience and turn-taking. The games need to be within the child's level of comprehension, and the game's result should be determined by chance so that the child can sometimes win. Show him/her how to 'lose gracefully'.

4 | Word games

This chapter provides a number of word games to encourage a child's language development and listening skills.

True or not true?

Say to the child, 'I am going to say some sentences to you. Listen carefully and after each sentence tell me whether it is true or not true.' Suggestions for sentences are as follows (some of these are purposefully ambiguous).

The TV is off.

We are sitting by the window.

Your legs bend.

A dog can fly.

Ducks can swim.

Bananas are pink.

A fire is hot.

Ice lollies are warm.

Milk is good to drink.

You are as big as Dad/Mum.

Apples can be blue.

You have one toe.

I wear glasses.

The supermarket sells food.

You are asleep.

Deliberate mistakes

Say to the child, 'I'm going to say some silly sentences. I'd like you to listen carefully. Tell me what is silly and suggest a more sensible sentence.' Suggestions for sentences are:

The dog said, 'Good morning'.

The tree sells bags of crisps.

The goldfish read the paper.

Katrina put her scarf on her feet.

The cat squeaked at the mouse.

Mum cleaned the carpet with the cookers.

The bus hopped down the road.

Michelle barked at the dog.

Paul turned on the basket and fried an egg.

Brett put on his pyjamas and went to play football.

The snow fell up onto the garden.

Jaishree wrapped her elephant round her neck to keep warm.

Mum closed the window to let in some fresh air.

The teacher opened the window and flew out.

Jason put his crayons away and drew a picture.

Riddles

Ask the child to complete the sentence. For example:

A person who takes care of sick people is a . . .

A person who helps children learn is a . . .

An animal with four legs that barks is a . . .

I swim in a pond and go 'quack'. I am a . . .

Sound game

This game encourages the child to listen carefully. There are two variations of the game and both need a tape of pre-recorded sounds and a tape recorder.

- **Paired sounds**: Explain to the child, 'I'm going to play two sounds. Listen carefully' (play the sounds). 'What do you think each sound was?'
  Examples of paired sounds could be:

motor bike/train	car/bus
car door/classroom door	class members' voices/musical instruments

- **Noise-making materials**: Follow the same procedure as for paired sounds. Examples could be:

scissors cutting paper   money chinking

tearing paper   pencil being sharpened

rattle   animal sounds

sand in a jar   closing a book

marbles in a jar

Tell me

Say to the child, 'We'll play "Tell me". I'll ask you questions and you tell me as much as you know. Tell me . . .

how you get home from school.

what you like about winter time.

what you would do if you had three wishes.

what you would do if you were suddenly changed into a dog.

why we wash ourselves.

why we eat.

why you go to school.

what you would notice at the seaside/at the shops.'

Sentence making

- Ask your child to make up sentences (simple but clearly expressed) using the following pairs of words:

paper/pencil	hard/ball
table/fork	car/fast
cooker/pan	telephone/speak
water/dishes	hungry/dinner
cup/coffee	school/late
sun/garden	tired/bed
cat/mouse	teacher/smiling
clean/basin	

● Ask the child to complete these sentences in his/her own words:

Kulvinder wore her best dress because . . .

Mr Brown could not get his car started so . . .

David's mother wanted to watch television so . . .

I like to fly my kite when . . .

The little white rabbit stays still in the woods because . . .

The frightened mouse ran when . . .

I was very angry with my brother because . . .

I dreamed that . . .

After tea I want to . . .

When Billy saw the horse it was . . .

● Make up a sentence but leave out one or two words and ask the child to supply the missing words, for example:

The shop was . . . so I went . . .

The boy sat on the . . . and . . .

Word fluency

Ask the child to name, in 30 seconds, as many animals, place names as he/she can.

Hypothetical situations

Ask the child, 'What would you do if you . . .', and then give them a hypothetical situation. For example:

. . . lost you door key?

. . . got lost in a big shop?

. . . went on holiday to the seaside?

The parent can ask the child to give as many solutions and alternatives to the situations as possible, not just the obvious ones.

Twenty questions

Present the child with a situation and say, 'You can ask me 20 questions to find out what I am.' (It can be made more difficult if you only answer with a 'Yes' or 'No'.) For example:

Child: What are you?

Adult: I'm an animal.

Child: Where do you live?

Adult: In the jungle.

or

Child: Are you an animal?

Adult: Yes.

Child: Do you live in the forest?

Adult: No.

Odd word out game (for listening)

Explain to the child, 'Listen to these words. Which one sounds different?' (read across)

hat	fat	cat	banana	mat
fan	man	mix	can	pan
red	bed	boy	fed	led
hill	pill	toy	fill	mill
Jill	spill	apple	bill	
pet	pig	jet	set	
cap	tap	sock	clap	
ring	bell	sing	spring	
look	book	top	took	
rub	hat	tub		

Describing

● Ask the child to give three words to describe any object the parent names, for example: ball. The child might say 'round, blue, bouncy'. Go on to ask the child, 'What is...for?' 'What do we do with...?'

● Ask the child to make up descriptive words for actions, such as: the wind blowing, a balloon bursting, rain falling.

5 | Acting and pretending

Acting and pretending are important aspects of children's play. Through role play children develop empathy with others, social understanding and greater imagination.

Pretending to telephone

Use a toy telephone if one is available. Say to the child, 'We're going to pretend to talk on the phone.' Decide on a scenario (some are outlined here) and decide who will play each part.

Scenario 1. Johnny has a bad stomach ache, so his mum telephones the doctor's surgery.

Receptionist: Good morning. Doctor Hooper's surgery. How can I help you?

Mum: Hello, this is Mrs Jones. My little boy is poorly and I'd like the doctor to see him please.

Receptionist: Can you get down to the surgery, or do you need the doctor to come to the house?

Mum: ...

Receptionist: ...

Scenario 2. Mary is late for school. Her teacher is worried and telephones Mary's mum.

Teacher: Hello, Mrs Murray, it's Mr Turner here, Mary's teacher. Mary hasn't got to school yet this morning and I was wondering if everything is all right.

Mum: Hello, Mr Turner. I'm not very well today so I have had to keep Mary at home this morning to look after ...

Teacher: ...

Mum: ...

Scenario 3. Grandma lives at the seaside and telephones her grandchild to invite him/her to stay.

Grandma: Hello, Ben, how are you today?

Ben: Hi, Gran, I'm fine, thank you.

Grandma: I was wondering if you would like to come and stay with me...

Ben: ...

Scenario 4. Michelle telephones her cousin Lena to thank her for her birthday present.

Michelle: Hi, Lena. I'm just phoning to thank you for my birthday present.

Lena: Hi, Michelle. Do you like it? Does it fit? What else did you get for your birthday?

Michelle: ...

Lena: ...

Acting out real-life scenes

Ask the child to enact the following situations with you. Decide who will play each part and encourage dialogue.

Scenario 1. Mum is at a parents' evening. John's teacher tells her how he is getting on and shows her some of his work.

Scenario 2. Peter and his friend, Amandeep, are in town looking at all the shops. They talk about what they can see and what they would like to buy.

Scenario 3. Susan and Ann are at the zoo. They talk about what they can see.

Scenario 4. Two friends have met at a bus stop. They have a chat about their favourite TV programmes.

Scenario 5. Mark and his mum are having breakfast before Mark has to go to school. They talk about going to the park and feeding the ducks after school.

Charades

Take turns to mime/guess the action. Examples of activities to mime: a person cleaning windows, chopping vegetables, driving a car, eating a meal, mopping the floor, washing dishes, hanging clothes on the line, having a bath, drinking, eating an apple, buttoning up a cardigan.

Miming and singing

Recite the rhyme 'This is the way...' and suggest common activities which can be mimed together, such as yawn, sweep, put on our socks, brush our hair, clean our teeth, put on our coats, jump out of bed, walk, eat our lunch.

This is the way...

This is the way we brush our teeth,

Brush our teeth, brush our teeth.

This is the way we brush our teeth

On a cold and frosty/warm and sunny morning...

Story mime

Take it in turns to mime a well-known story sequence and ask each other, in turn, what is happening. Examples of stories that can be used are:

Cinderella trying on the glass slipper;

Goldilocks being woken by the three bears;

Jack stealing the goose from the giant.

6 | Using the five senses

Encouraging children to use their senses offers a range of learning experiences. Listening, in particular, is an important skill necessary for language development. Furthermore, these experiences provide an opportunity for children to extend their vocabulary.

Hearing and listening

The silence game

Adult and child listen for periods of 10 or 15 seconds reporting to each other what each has heard.

Variation in voice levels

- Whisper a simple statement or message to the child who then repeats it to you, or someone else.
- Vary the level of your voice when telling or reading a story.
- Try out different voices to be used in different situations, for example sitting close together, calling from the kitchen, shouting into the garden from the doorway.

Listen carefully

Tell the child, 'I want you to listen for a number. When you hear it touch my arm.' Then say the words from one of the rows in the lists below allowing the child time to respond before moving on to another row. Try with animals, child's names, colours etc. (If you develop your own lists of words note that the words in each group need not rhyme with each other.)

Number

tree	me	three	free		live	dive	hive	five
pen	hen	ten	when		sticks	six	trick	lick
shoe	chew	two	who		run	one	bun	fun
late	eight	date	hate		more	chore	four	war

Animal

log	fog	cog	dog		take	make	cake	snake
pig	fig	dig	wig		course	sauce	horse	force
how	now	cow	bow		Sam	ham	cam	lamb
sheep	sleep	deep	keep		scowl	growl	prowl	owl

Count the words

Explain to the child, 'I'm going to say lots of words. Listen carefully, and each time I say a food word say the word loudly after me. At the end we'll count out how many food words there were.' Then say a list of words including some items of food, for example:

box, carpet, stairs, eggs, car, bag, potatoes.

Instruction

Give the child a range of instructions beginning with one-sequence requests, for example, 'Bring your book to me please', through to a several-sequence request, such as, 'Go to the top drawer and get me your blue socks.' The complexity of the sequence can vary according to the child. The activity can be repeated with the child requesting the adult to do similar things.

List games

Ask the child to memorise a list, for example, 'I am going to put on my brown shoes...and my white socks...and my blue scarf...' At the end each child has to remember how he/she is supposed to be dressed. Variations of this could be:

'I went to the park and saw a...and a...'
'In my house there are...and...and...'
'In my school there is...and...and...'

Smelling

Smell different objects

The parent and child move around the house smelling different objects and comparing sensations and impressions.

Likes and dislikes

List the smells you both like and dislike, for example flowers, wood, plants, petrol, vegetables etc. Variations of this could be to list smells that could be a sign of danger, such as gas, or burning, or smells that accompany actions or events, for example car exhaust, or food cooking.

Touching

Feely bags

Put one object at a time into a cloth or plastic carrier bag, without the child seeing it. Ask the child to feel it in the bag. Describe how it feels and guess what the object is.

Describing textiles

Ask the child to close their eyes and present them with a range of everyday household objects with different textures (sponge, flannel, sandpaper, plastic spoon, cotton wool). Encourage the child to use a variety of descriptive words, such as rough, smooth, heavy, cold etc.

Looking

'I spy' game

Say, for example, 'I spy, with my little eye, something...

    made of wood;

    that you write with;

    blue beginning with a "p".'.

Classification

Say to the child, 'Look around and tell me everything that is...(red, round, made of glass, begins with an 's').'

Open-ended questions

Ask the child open-ended questions (see Key points 2), for example:

'What do you notice about that box?'

'What's different between this chair and that chair?'

Looking together at books and pictures can provide material to prompt open-ended questions (see Chapter 2 on story and picture books).

Cooking

Preparing food is a good way to allow children to experience different tastes and textures and feel that they are being helpful. It also creates lots of opportunities for conversation.

Stirring and mixing: Yoghurt dishes are a good idea. Provide some plain yoghurt and let the child stir in some raisins/chopped fruit/jam/honey or chocolate chips. Instant cake mixes are also very simple to use. Put a damp cloth under the mixing bowl to stop it slipping.

Cutting and spreading: This can be practised using a round-edged, blunt knife. Use soft foods to cut at first – bananas, mushrooms, sliced bread. Have a selection of different shaped cutters for making biscuits, scones and fancy sandwiches. Spread margarine/jam/chocolate spread/soft cheese/marmite.

Rolling out: Use pastry/bread/biscuit dough, scone mix or ready-made fondant icing for cakes (use a little food colouring to paint on the child's initial or a simple design).

Decorating: This can make food more appealing to children. Some ideas are: icing cakes and biscuits (with cherries, chocolate buttons etc. on top); garnishing savoury dishes with parsley or watercress; 'hundreds and thousands' or grated chocolate on a trifle.

Making a pizza: Use a ready-made base and a choice of ingredients. After cooking, compare tastes.

Tasting

Talking about tastes is best done during food preparation (for some ideas see opposite) or mealtimes. The main aim is to encourage the child to talk about tastes, smells, textures and changes in appearance of food as it is being prepared (see Chapter 1 on food, p. 21).

Using the senses to develop understanding of safety

At home

The adult asks the child questions about safety in the home to encourage discussion, such as, 'What would you do if you smelled something burning?' Other topics for discussion could include sources of danger to children, such as stairs, lifts, getting lost at the shops.

Using the senses to develop road safety

It would be helpful for these activities to have pictures and/or models of vehicles. (Some local authorities have road safety packs.)

(a) With accompanying materials, talk about different sorts of vehicles, their purpose, their sounds, who drives them. Example: bicycles, motorbikes, cars, vans, post vans, lorries, buses, fire engines, ambulances, tractors.

(b) Talk about key words to do with traffic, safety and dangers, for example: pavements, kerbs, corners, traffic islands, parking and parked cars, bus stops, playing in safe places, using pedestrian crossings. Stress the importance of using eyes and ears to look and listen when crossing the road.

(c) Use toys and models to construct road scenes and enact common scenarios. Make up stories which will encourage your child to think about road safety. Include road safety points in other storytelling.

7 | Thinking, remembering and reasoning

These activities are designed to help the child acquire and remember information more effectively. They will also help the child to think flexibly and develop problem-solving skills.

Remembering

- Place a few objects in a line and ask the child to name them. Jumble the objects up into a different order and ask the child to put them back as they were.

- Play 'Kim's game' by placing a number of objects on a table. The child says aloud what they are, then closes his or her eyes and the parent removes one object. The child then looks at the remaining objects and tries to identify which object has been removed. Make it harder by removing more than one object and/or using more objects.

- The parent moves around the room touching several objects while the child watches. The parent says, 'Can you remember which things I touched?'

- Play a secret code memory game. At the beginning of the session, give the child a 'secret code' of one sentence length. The sentences can vary in length and complexity according to the age of the child:

    'The cat walked along the wall.'

    'Monica liked to eat a big red apple before she went to school every day.'

    Ask the child to repeat it at the end of the session.

Lateral thinking

General brainstorming

Say to the child, 'How many things can we do with a brick?' (build houses, make a shelf, a step). Instead of a brick you could use one of the following: stick, tin, brush, bath, bucket, box, piece of paper, matchbox.

Finding links

Ask the child to find a relationship between apparently unrelated things. For example, 'How are a postman's bag and a school satchel alike?' or 'How are a library and a newsagent's alike?'

Use riddles and rhymes

Encourage the child to make up simple riddles and rhymes, for example: an animal that rhymes with a log; a thing you read which rhymes with look; a flower which rhymes with hose; a building you live in which rhymes with mouse; an animal that rhymes with mat; a part of your body which rhymes with land.

Classification

Ask the child to:

- tell you everything that comes in tins, glass jars, bottles;
- name everything that has buttons, tails, legs, wheels;
- name as many of the following as possible: boys' and girls' names, colours, food, things you do in school, in the streets, park.

Logical comprehension

Making inferences

Tell short stories with inferences for the child to work out. For example:

- The teacher gave everyone in the class a note to take home to give to their parents. The note reminded parents about a school trip the next day. All the children had to come to school very early, by eight o'clock the next morning.

When Timothy arrived at school the next morning at the usual time nobody was there. What do you think happened?

● Mrs Harris had just put some cakes in the oven to bake when the telephone rang. She went to answer the phone. It was her friend Molly. They chatted for a long time. After a while her son Danny came home from school. 'Mum,' he called out, 'there's a funny burning smell.' What do you think it was? What happened next?

Similar and dissimilar comparisons

● Ask the child, 'How are a bus and a car alike? How are they different?' Develop the theme, if the child appears not to understand, for example: 'Well, what do you do in a bus, a car?' Other comparisons could be:

water, milk	spade, bucket	dog, cat
fly, ant	bat, ball	pen, pencil
torch, lamp-post	salt, sauce	nail, screw
carrot, onion	knife, spoon	boy, man
stamp, letter	pilot, engine driver	plate, tray
garage, bus depot	chair, table	radio, TV
cricket ball, football		

● Compare objects for texture, colour, size, shape, weight, function, pebbles, sand, water, toys, bricks. Ask the child, 'What is the difference between the pebble and the sweet?' 'Why is a ball like a marble?'

● Draw the child's attention to similar aspects of things: 'A ball is round; an orange is round.' Conversely, point out differences: 'An elephant is large; a mouse is small'; 'A lake is deep; a puddle is shallow'.

● Encourage the child to make analogies (like and unlike), for example say:

'Aeroplanes fly, boats…'   'A rabbit runs quickly, a tortoise walks…'

'Water is drunk, food is…'   'Grass is green, violets are…'

'Bricks are heavy, feathers are…'   'It is dark at night, but in daytime it is…'

'A cat runs , a kangaroo…'   'A dog has puppies, a cat has…'

'A trumpet blasts, a drum…'   'Walls are thick, paper is…'

Comparatives

Ask the child to complete the sentences, giving them the example first to show them the comparative.

A river is deep, the sea is (deeper).

A house is big, a school is . . .

A lorry is long, a train is even . . .

A dog is furry, a bear is even . . .

A kite flies high, an aeroplane flies . . .

A tree is tall, a mountain is . . .

Opposites

Explain to the child, if necessary, what an opposite is, using examples. Then, taking a word from the list below, say, 'Tell me the opposite of . . .' and 'Make up a sentence with the word in it'.

empty	heavy	crowded
sweet	push	fast
long	hungry	brother
large	always	sometimes
front	help	young
high	light	busy
noise	early	warm
soft	happy	friendly
quickly	many	morning

Cause and effect

The aim of these activities is to develop understanding of actions and events and their consequences. Some of the activities are concerned with events and phenomena and others with social situations and social interaction. Ask the child questions such as those listed here and encourage the child to elaborate on their replies.

- Why?: 'Can you tell me why...

  we sleep?

  we eat?

  we come to school?

  we wear clothes?

  you would walk slowly carrying a tray of cakes?

  you would not rush across the road without looking?

  you wouldn't wear a raincoat on a hot, sunny day?

  you sleep on a bed, and not on the floor or in a chair?'

- If: 'What would you do if...

  a ball you were playing with bounced on to the busy road?

  you lost some money on your way to buy some groceries for Mum?

  you spilt some milk on the carpet at home?

  you had two sweets and a friend had none?

  you were hungry?

  you were cold in bed at night?

  you lost a favourite toy?

  you lost a favourite toy belonging to a friend?

  you lost a coat at school?

- Social cause and effect:

  'Peter broke his cup. What did his mother say?'

  'Mother lost her purse. What did she do?'

  'Jane was crying. Why?'

  'Jill and Sally had a quarrel. Why?'

- Because:

  'John was off to school because...'

  'Jenny was late home from the park because...'

  'The car stopped at the side of the road because...'

  'Tom's father rushed to the telephone because...'

  'Mary burst into tears because...'

  'Paul and Peter had a quarrel because...'

  'Michelle was laughing with Marie because...'

8 | Awareness of time

Here is a list of suggested activities to develop a child's awareness of time and introduce new words associated with it.

- Develop the child's awareness of seasons, months, days and weeks by using large calendars and time lines. Make the child's birthday special and mark off days on the calendar coming up to holidays and special treats.

- Make use of a clock or watch to show the passing of time, for example:

    'When the big hand turns round to the 3, it will be time to go out and meet Evie from school.' 'When my watch shows 19.00 it's time to get ready for bed.'

- Remember special events and days out by talking, drawing pictures, using materials collected (shells, leaves, conkers).

- Discuss plans for the day/next day/next week and use the appropriate 'time words' – tomorrow, today, next Monday.

- Before any trip or visit, talk with the child about what will happen and what he/she is likely to see and hear.

- Talk about what happened yesterday, last week, last year – looking at photographs is a good way of remembering past events. For example: 'Do you remember when we went to the seaside in the summer holidays last year?'

- Common time words can be incorporated into conversations and stories such as: during, after, before, end, beginning, always, never, sometimes, first, last, early, late, occasionally, often.

- Encourage the child to think about time:

    'When do we brush our teeth?' 'We brush our teeth twice a day, once in the morning and once before we go to bed.'

    'Shall we go to the park before lunch or after lunch?

A diagram such as the one overleaf can provide a focus for discussion about different times of the day.

24 hours in a day

Evening

Morning

Afternoon

9 | Language of number, quantity, position, size and measurement

Remember to use these words frequently so that the child becomes familiar with them and what they mean (see the word list overleaf). Simple counting games and rhymes can be useful (and fun!), for example, 'One, two, three, four, five, Once I caught a fish alive...'

Straight and curved lines

Using a pencil and paper, say to the child, 'Let's draw a straight line. Now let's draw a curved, rounded line. Let's think of some things that have straight lines, or are straight, then some things that are round.' Use hand demonstration as reminders. Encourage the child to think of examples by providing clues if necessary.

Straight objects	Curved, rounded objects	Objects that can be both
knife, book, table, door, wall, pencil	ball, orange, banana, apple, moon, plate, saucer	chair, spoons, flower

Liquids

Ask the child:

'What is a liquid?' (Encourage the child to think how a liquid can be distinguished from a solid.)

'Let's think of some liquids.' (water, milk, beer, squash, pop, perfume, washing-up liquid, medicines in bottles)

'What can be added to water to make a tasty drink?' (orange, lemon, tea, coffee)

'Let's think of some things that can hold liquid.' (sink, bath, bucket, bowl, tank, bottle, vase, cup, can, jug, measuring jug)

Word list

above	half	pair
after	heavy (ier) (iest)	
ahead of	high (er) (est)	quarter
all		
almost	in	right
apart	in front of	
around	inside	second
as many as		several
	large (r) (est)	short (er) (est)
backwards	last	small (er) (est)
beginning	least	some
behind	left	
below	less than	tall (er) (est)
beside	light (er) (est)	third
between	little	three
bottom	long (er) (est)	top
	lower	towards
down		two
	middle	
each	more than	under
empty	most	underneath
end		up
equal	narrow (er) (est)	upper
every	near (er) (est)	
		whole
far(ther) (thest)	next to (position)	
few (er) (est)	next (sequence)	zero
first	nought	
five		
forward(s)	one	
four	out	
full	over	
further (furthest)		

References and suggested further reading

Basic Skills Agency (2002) *Read with Me: A Guide for Parents and Children* (in English and Welsh). BSA, Commonwealth House, 1-19, New Oxford St, London WC1A 1NU.

Branston, P. and Provis, M. (1999) *Children and Parents Enjoying Reading.* London: David Fulton Publishers.

Desforges, C. and Abouchar, A. (2003) *The Impact of Parental Involvement, Parental Support and Family Education on Pupil Achievement and Adjustment: A Literature Review* (Research Report No. 433). London: Department for Education and Skills.

Fox, C. (1993) *At the Very Edge of the Forest: The Influence of Literature on Storytelling by Children.* London: Cassell.

National Literacy Trust and Department for Education and Skills (2002) *Getting a Headstart: A Good Ideas Guide for Promoting Reading to Young Families.* NLT, Swire House, 59 Buckingham Gate, London SW1E 6AJ. www.literacytrust.org.uk

Nutbrown, C., Hannon, P. and Morgan, A. (2005) *Early Literacy Work with Families: Policy, Practice and Research.* London: Sage Publications.

Palmer, S. and Bayley, R. (2004) *Foundations of Literacy: A Balanced Approach to Language, Listening and Literacy Skills in the Early Years.* Stafford: Network Educational Press.

Qualifications and Curriculum Authority (2003) *Foundation Stage Profile Handbook.* Ref. QCA/03/1006. QCA, 83 Piccadilly, London W1J 8QA. www.qca.org.uk

Wade, B. and Moore, M. (2000) *Baby Power.* Cheshire: Egmont Publishing.

Ward, S. (2000) *Babytalk.* London: Century/Random House.

Whitehead, M. (2004) *Language and Literacy in the Early Years,* 3rd edition. London: Paul Chapman.

Wolfendale, S. and Topping, K. (eds) (1996) *Family Involvement in Literacy: Effective Partnerships in Education*. London: Cassell.

Wolfendale, S. and Bastiani, J. (eds) (2000) *The Contribution of Parents to School Effectiveness*. London: David Fulton Publishers.

See also, the National Literacy Association at www.nla.org.uk

Index